salads

FIRST IN THE SERIES: ANNIE'S ELEGANT, DELICIOUS COOKING

Kami,
I hope you have fun
with these recipes.

Best Wishes,

Annie Simensen

annie simensen

Table of Contents

Introduction

Salads, is the first book in the series: *Annie's Elegant, Delicious Cooking*. I wrote this series of books to help people who enjoy cooking and entertaining to prepare visually appealing and mouthwateringly delicious dishes in their own kitchens from food and produce available in an average American supermarket. All of the recipes in this series are those I use every day for my family, friends and guests. Many of the dishes I originally developed for the international students at my Singapore cooking school. None of my recipes require special culinary training or expertise. Besides a refrigerator, oven, cook-top and the usual kitchen appliances, a quality, mini-food processor, a 14-cup food processor and blender are the only other necessities.

Salads appear on the table in varying combinations and at different times of the meal. In American restaurants and homes, salads are often the starting course for a dinner, but in French, Italian and other European cuisines, salads often appear toward the middle or the end of a dinner service. Some of the salads in this volume are intended as main courses; with others, the addition of sliced chicken, shrimp or meats can transform a basic salad into an easy to prepare, hearty meal.

Few of us today have the space or time to maintain a salad garden; I certainly don't. Fortunately for us, the average American supermarket has a year-round profusion of the fresh ingredients these recipes require.

A salad bowl is the perfect canvas for experimentation and creativity. Once you've mastered the basics, try personalizing my salads with your own favorite garnishes or additions. Have fun with these elegant, delicious salads.

Antipasti Salad

This fills a very large platter and can be used as a buffet dish or as a complete lunch.

Ingredients

1 head of your favorite lettuce (*I use Romaine because it's flavorful and doesn't wilt easily*)

6 campari tomatoes, washed and quartered

2-5 oz. cans albacore tuna fish, drained

1-14 oz. can or jar marinated artichoke hearts, drained and quartered

8-12 slices Genoa Salami, cut into quarters

8 -12 slices Prosciutto, cut into 1 inch pieces

12 red radishes, washed

30 Kalamata olives, pitted

Dressing

1 cup good quality extra virgin olive oil

1 – 2 oz. can flat anchovies, well drained

4 Tablespoons fresh lemon juice

Pepper, to taste

Directions

1. Tear the lettuce into bite-sized pieces, wash and spin dry.

2. Get out a large platter and line it with the prepared lettuce.

3. Arrange the antipasti.

4. Mix all of the dressing ingredients in a food processor or blender for 10 seconds.

5. You can either pour the dressing evenly over the salad or serve it in a pitcher on the side.

I sometimes sprinkle a little freshly chopped parsley over the whole salad.

Arugula, Tomato & Mozzarella Salad

Arugula usually comes in a rectangular shaped plastic tub. It is sometimes called "rocket" and has a fresh peppery taste. This salad is quick to put together and is always popular.

Ingredients

4 cups arugula, washed and spun dried
(Please remove all of the larger stems)

4 large, very ripe red tomatoes,
sliced 1/3 inch thick

16 ounces mozzarella cheese, sliced
1/3 inch thick

1/4 cup extra virgin olive oil

Kosher salt and freshly ground peppercorns

Directions

1. Place the prepared arugula in the <u>middle</u> of a large round platter.

2. Around the edges of the platter alternate slices of the tomatoes and mozzarella.

3. Sprinkle everything on the platter with kosher salt and freshly ground peppercorns and then drizzle with 1/4 cup extra virgin olive oil.

If I can't find good ripe regular tomatoes, I buy the campari type, which are always ripe. And since they are smaller, I may use about 10 of them.

Avocado, Mandarin Orange & Arugula Salad

You could peel and slice fresh oranges, but it's easier to open a can of mandarin orange segments.

Ingredients

2 ripe Haas avocados, peeled, pitted and sliced

Juice of 1 lemon *(which is 2 to 3 tablespoons)**

1 - 15 oz. can Mandarin orange segments, drained *(Please reserve 3 Tablespoons of the juice)*

6 cups (4 oz.) fresh arugula, rinsed and dried in salad spinner

1/4 cup very thinly sliced peeled red onion

Dressing

1 cup sour cream *(not light or low fat)*

3 Tablespoons white wine vinegar

3 Tablespoons reserved Mandarin orange juice

3 Tablespoons good mayonnaise *(I use Hellmann's)*

1 teaspoon granulated sugar

Directions

1. Mix all of the dressing ingredients in a bowl *(not metal)* and stir with a fork or whisk until well blended.

2. Arrange the arugula, avocado slices, mandarin oranges and red onion on a round shallow glass or ceramic platter.

3. Drizzle a little of the dressing over the top and place a pitcher with the rest of the sauce on the side.

As soon as you have prepared the avocado slices, dip each slice into the lemon juice and place on a plate until you are ready to arrange the salad. This step is important. It will prevent the slices from turning brown.

Dip avocado slices in lemon juice to prevent them from turning brown.

Baby Spinach Salad with Gorgonzola Cheese & Warm Sliced Sauteed Baby Bella Mushrooms

Ingredients

1 – 6 oz. bag baby spinach leaves
(Please wash and spin dry)

5 oz. Gorgonzola cheese, sliced

16 oz. fresh baby bella mushrooms
(pre-sliced)

2 Tablespoons extra virgin olive oil

Dressing

(Please do not mix ingredients together)

2 teaspoons good balsamic vinegar

4 Tablespoons extra virgin olive oil

A little Kosher salt for sprinkling

Directions

1. Divide spinach between 4 salad plates.

2. Place the Gorgonzola slices on top of the spinach.

3. Sauté the mushrooms in a little extra virgin olive oil for 5-6 minutes until tender.

4. Spoon the mushrooms evenly over the plates.

5. Sprinkle a tiny amount of balsamic vinegar over each plate.

6. Sprinkle 1 Tablespoon extra virgin olive oil over each plate.

7. And finally, sprinkle a pinch of Kosher salt over each plate.

Black Olive Salad

Ingredients

1 can jumbo pitted black olives *(It says 6 oz. drained on the can. So just drain them and you will have the right amount)*

30 pitted Kalamata olives

30 oil-cured black olives*

1/4 cup chopped fresh parsley

2 Tablespoons chopped fresh rosemary

3 Tablespoons chopped fresh basil

1 Tablespoon chopped fresh oregano

5 cloves garlic, peeled and chopped finely

3 Tablespoons extra virgin olive oil

Kosher salt and freshly ground pepper

Directions

1. Mix all of the olives together in a large glass serving dish.

2. Put all of the herbs and garlic in a mini food processor and chop until fine.

3. Add these herbs to the olives and stir.

4. Sprinkle the extra virgin olive oil, Kosher salt and pepper over the olives and stir well. Start with a little of the salt and pepper and taste. You might want more.

5. You can refrigerate these or just serve them at room temperature.

Oil cured black olives look wrinkly. They come in a jar with pits, which are difficult to remove. I leave them in and just warn people.

Caesar Salad

Ingredients

2 small to medium sized heads of Romaine lettuce hearts

3 Tablespoons extra virgin olive oil

3/4 cup freshly grated Parmesan cheese

Juice of 1 lime

4 shakes Worcestershire Sauce

1 teaspoon seasoned garlic salt *(I use Lawry's)*

3/4 teaspoon Coleman's dried mustard

1/4 teaspoon freshly ground peppercorns

1 - 2 oz. can anchovy fillets, drained and chopped coarsely

1 large or extra-large egg

1 cup bought croutons

Directions

1. Core the lettuce and tear into bite-sized pieces. Wash and spin dry. Place in large shallow wooden serving bowl. Place in fridge until you're ready to dress the salad.

2. I place all of the other ingredients in small dishes and arrange them all on the table with the cooled lettuce.

3. Crack the egg and beat it with a fork in a bowl.

4. Tip all of your ingredients onto the salad and toss.

Just skip the anchovies if you don't like them. Also, I sometimes substitute a good blue cheese for the parmesan.

Caviar Pasta Salad

This salad uses the lumpfish roe which you can find in small, 2 oz. glass jars in the canned fish section of the supermarket. You can usually find red, yellow or black roe. Here I use the red and yellow.

Ingredients

1 - 2 oz. jar red lumpfish roe, drained

1 - 2 oz jar yellow lumpfish roe, drained

8 oz. very small ditalini dried pasta

1-1/4 cups good mayonnaise
(I use Hellman's)

1-1/4 cups sour cream
(not light or low fat)

1/3 cup light cream *(not whipped)*

Directions

1. Cook the pasta in boiling salted water until <u>completely</u> tender.

2. Drain the pasta in a colander and rinse with cold water. Shake the colander to get rid of excess water.

3. In a large glass bowl, stir the mayonnaise, sour cream and light cream together until well blended.

4. Add the cooked pasta and stir until blended.

5. Just before serving, stir in the "caviar". Please do not use the juices which are in each jar. Stir very carefully so you don't accidentally smash the "caviar".

I don't add extra salt because the roe is salty enough.

This is a meal all by itself.

Chef's Salad

All of these ingredients are sitting next to each other, but not mixed together. It's much more attractive this way and your family and guests can choose what they want. Get out a very large platter.

Ingredients

1 bag spring mix greens, washed and spun dried

6-8 Campari tomatoes, washed and cut into quarters

1 hot house cucumber, sliced into 1/3 inch slices *(You can avoid peeling because the peel is thin)*

1 red pepper, seeded and cut into thin slices

1 yellow or orange pepper, seeded, cut into thin slices

30 pitted Kalamata olives

8 oz. jar marinated artichoke hearts, drained and cut into 1 inch chunks

1/2 lb. Fontina cheese, cut into small strips

1/3 lb. good blue cheese, crumbled

1 large chicken breast, roasted and cut into 1 inch cubes

1/3 lb. Prosciutto, sliced thinly, roll each slice into a "cigar"

1/3 lb. Sopressata, sliced thinly

4-6 hard boiled eggs, peeled and quartered

Commercial creamy balsamic dressing

Directions

1. Line the very large platter with the prepared greens.

2. Arrange all of the other prepared ingredients in a spiral on the greens.

3. Drizzle balsamic dressing evenly over the top.

Chicken Salad

This salad tastes amazingly good, looks delicious and makes a beautiful complete lunch. Just add an artisan loaf of unsliced bread and some good butter.

Ingredients

Green lettuce leaves and radicchio leaves for lining your platter

4-5 cups cooked chicken breast and thigh meat, cut into small bite sized cubes *(Make sure you remove all bones)*

1 small can Mandarin Orange segments, drained

1-1/2 cups seedless green grapes, washed and halved

3/4 teaspoon salt

1/4 teaspoon finely ground white pepper

1/2 teaspoon dried mustard *(I use Coleman's)*

3/4 cup sour cream, not light or low fat

3/4 cup good mayonnaise *(I use Hellmann's)*

3/4 cup chopped pecans, lighted toasted in sauté pan

1/2 cup very finely diced celery
(I use the inner stalks)

Directions

1. Line a large platter with both lettuce leaves, alternating

2. Mix remaining ingredients together in a large glass bowl

3. Place this on your prepared platter

Cobb Salad

This is a beautiful to look at and incredibly easy to make salad. Assemble everything on a very large rectangular glass or ceramic platter.

Ingredients

Red radishes

Good quality blue cheese, crumbled

1/3 lb. cooked crumbled bacon

Sliced scallions

Quartered campari tomatoes

Diced cooked chicken or turkey

Quartered hard boiled eggs

Commercial guacamole

Directions

Line the whole platter with washed Boston lettuce leaves or any other lettuce that you like. You decide on the quantities. I serve this with a good quality commercial ranch dressing.

Cranberry Salad Mold

Ingredients

1 cup water

1 - 20 oz. can crushed pineapple, drained, save 1 cup juice

1 - 3 oz. package raspberry jello

1 - 3 oz. package orange jello

1 - 14 oz. can <u>whole</u> cranberry sauce, Ocean Spray brand

1 - 6 oz. can frozen orange juice concentrate, thawed, Minute Maid brand

2 inner ribs of celery, destrung and diced into tiny pieces

Garnish

1-1/4 cups uncooked raw fresh cranberries

Directions

Use a 6-cup Tupperware mold. Spray with "Pam".

1. Bring water and reserved juice to boil in a medium to large saucepan then remove from heat.

2. Stir in the raspberry and orange jello. Stir until well dissolved.

3. Add the pineapple, cranberry sauce, orange juice concentrate and diced celery. Mix well.

4. Pour this into your prepared mold and place in the fridge for 4 hours or overnight.

5. Dip the bottom of the mold <u>quickly</u> in hot water. If you are using a Tupperware mold just release the inner seal.

6. Turn upside down and place on your serving plate.

7. Keep the salad in the refrigerator until ready to serve.

8. Place the raw cranberries in a small ramekin and place in the middle of the salad.

Cucumber Salad

Ingredients

2 Hot House cucumbers*

1/4 cup fresh dill weed, stems removed and <u>finely</u> minced

7 scallions, sometimes called green onions, roots removed and washed. (*Use all of white part and 3 inches of the green part. Slice thinly*)

1/2 teaspoon celery salt

1/2 teaspoon dried mustard

1/4 teaspoon ground white pepper

Dressing

1-1/2 cups sour cream

1 cup plain yogurt (*I use Greek*)

2 Tablespoons white wine vinegar

1-1/2 Tablespoons sugar

3/4 teaspoon salt

Directions

1. Take the plastic off of the cucumbers, cut a little off each end and discard. Slice the cucumbers in very thin slices. Use the food processor for this. It's so much quicker.

2. Place all of the slices and the next 5 ingredients in a large glass bowl. Mix well, but gently.

3. In another glass bowl, stir all of the dressing ingredients together

4. Pour the dressing over the cucumber mix and stir gently until well mixed.

5. Transfer to a pretty glass or ceramic bowl and cover tightly with plastic wrap.

Hot House cucumbers are also called European cucumbers. They are always wrapped in plastic wrap, are long and quite skinny, with very few seeds.

Curried Chicken Salad

Ingredients

2-3 cooked boneless chicken breasts
(Cut these into 1/2 inch cubes)

1/2 medium sized yellow onion, peeled
and grated to a pulp

2 inner ribs of celery, cut into very small dice

1 small can pineapple tid-bits, drained

1 cup good mayonnaise, not reduced fat
or light *(I use Hellman's)*

1/2 cup light or heavy cream

1 Tablespoon ginger paste *(comes in
a tube in the herb section of a good
supermarket)*

1-1/2 Tablespoons curry powder

Garnish

1 cup mango jam

Fresh lettuce leaves

Directions

1. Place the curry powder in a small Teflon
    sauté pan. Over medium heat, stir the
    curry powder for about 1 minute until
    you can smell the aroma. Take this off
    the heat right away. Burnt curry powder
    doesn't taste very good!

2. Now place all of the ingredients. except
    the mango jam, in a large glass bowl and
    stir until the chicken is well coated.

3. I serve these in individual lettuce "cups"
    with the mango jam in a separate bowl in
    the middle of the platter.

I serve these in individual lettuce "cups".

This is perfect as a dessert or for a fancy brunch.

Fresh Fruit Salad Platter

Ingredients

Fresh kiwi slices

Fresh blackberries

Fresh pineapple chunks

Fresh Raspberries

Fresh Blueberries

Fresh whole Strawberries

Fresh cherries

Slices of fresh cantaloupe

Directions

Arrange all of the washed, peeled, hulled and pitted fruit in their own "compartment". Please don't mix them together. Serve commercial crème fraiche or plain yogurt on the side as a dressing.

I use this also as a dessert for a large crowd and as an addition to a fancy brunch. Please feel free to substitute your own favorite fruits.

Green Salad

This is a thoroughly delicious accompaniment to almost any meal.

Ingredients

6-8 cups "Spring mix" greens, washed and spun dried

3/4 cup walnut pieces, warmed for a minute in a sauté pan

3/4 cup sun-dried cherries
(they are already pitted)

4 oz. good quality blue cheese, crumbled

1/4 cup thinly sliced red onion *(make sure you peel it first)*

Dressing

2 Tablespoons extra virgin olive oil

1/2 teaspoon balsamic vinegar

salt and freshly ground peppercorns to taste

Directions

1. Gently toss all of the salad ingredients together in a glass or ceramic serving bowl.

2. Drizzle the extra virgin olive oil and the balsamic vinegar over the top of the salad.

3. Sprinkle some salt and pepper over the salad and <u>toss</u> gently.

4. Taste the salad now to see if you want more salt or pepper.

Put the dressing on the salad just before you're ready to serve. You don't want the greens to get soggy.

You can serve this either cold or at room temperature.

Gutsy Potato Salad

Ingredients

3 lbs. red skinned potatoes, washed, not peeled and cut into bite-sized chunks.

1/2 cup extra virgin olive oil

5 Campari tomatoes, washed and cut into sixths

20 pitted Kalamata black olives, halved

1 regular American cucumber, peeled, seeded and cubed

8 leaves fresh basil, thinly sliced

2 Tablespoons capers, rinsed with water and drained

4 Tablespoons white champagne vinegar

3 hard boiled eggs, peeled and cut into sixths lengthwise

Salt and freshly ground white peppercorns to taste

Directions

We're using extra virgin olive oil here as our dressing. No mayonnaise is required. You can serve this cold or at room temperature.

1. Cook potato chunks in boiling salted water until tender *(but _not_ falling apart)*. This will take 10-15 minutes.

2. Drain cooked potato chunks and place in a large glass bowl.

3. Add all of the other ingredients and mix _gently_ with a large spoon. Try not to squash the potatoes, tomatoes or eggs.

Iceberg Lettuce Wedges with Gorgonzola Cheese and Bacon

Ingredients

1 good-sized head of iceberg lettuce, outer wilted leaves removed and cut into 6 wedges

6 oz. Gorgonzola Blue Cheese, crumbled

1/2 lb. bacon, cooked until crisp, drained and crumbled

1 very small Vidalia onion, peeled, halved and sliced very thinly

2/3 – 3/4 cup commercial creamy balsamic dressing *(I use Paul Newman's)*

Directions

1. Arrange the wedges on 6 pretty dishes or plates.

2. Sprinkle even amounts of cheese, bacon and onion slices on each wedge.

3. Pour about 1-1/2 Tablespoons dressing over each wedge.

This salad gets better as it sits.

Macaroni Salad

Ingredients

1/2 lb. dried "elbow" macaroni pasta,
<u>fully</u> cooked and drained

3 inner ribs of celery, destrung and cut into
tiny pieces

1 medium sized yellow onion, peeled and
chopped <u>very</u> finely with the chopping blade
of a food processor

2 cups "grape" tomatoes, washed and halved

3/4 cup pitted Kalamata black olives, halved

3 cups good quality mayonnaise thinned
with 1/2 cup milk

Salt and freshly ground white peppercorns
to taste

Directions

1. Place completely cooked pasta in a large
   glass bowl.

2. Add all of the other ingredients. Stir gently
   with a large spoon.

3. Taste for flavor and add more salt or
   pepper if needed.

4. Cover bowl tightly with plastic wrap and
   refrigerate until needed.

*This salad can be made the day before you
need it.*

Orzo Salad

This salad is wonderful. It has a Greek nature to it and is very satisfying as well as being healthy.

Ingredients

1/2 lb. (8 oz. or 1 cup) dried orzo *(a tiny, rice shaped pasta)*

8 oz. fresh baby spinach *(rinsed and spun dried)*

1/2 medium sized red onion, peeled

7 scallions, roots cut off. Use all of the white part and 3 inches of the green part

6 oz Feta cheese, crumbled *(the kind that's packed in water is the best)*

3/4 cup pine nuts *(quickly sautéed in a sauté pan until slightly golden brown)*

zest and juice of 1 large lemon

1/3 cup extra virgin olive oil

Directions

1. Cook the orzo pasta in boiling salted water until tender to the taste. Drain.

2. Place this pasta in a large glass bowl.

3. Chop the raw spinach, red onion and prepared scallions together in the food processor.

4. Add this mixture to the bowl with the pasta.

5. Now add all of the remaining ingredients to the bowl and stir gently with a large spoon until thoroughly mixed.

6. Cover the bowl with plastic wrap and keep refrigerated until you're ready to serve.

44

Pasta Salad with Basil Pesto Sauce

Please feel free to buy pesto instead of making it from scratch. You can find it in the fresh pasta section of your supermarket.

Ingredients

1/2 lb (8 oz.) dried mini penne pasta

2 cups basil pesto sauce

3/4-1 cup extra virgin olive oil

3/4 cup lightly toasted pine nuts

1 cup freshly grated Parmesan cheese

Directions

1. Cook pasta in boiling salted water until tender. Drain and transfer to a large glass bowl.

2. Add the pesto, extra virgin olive oil, pine nuts and Parmesan to your cooked pasta.

2. Mix gently with a large spoon. Be careful not to crush the pasta.

3. Transfer to a large shallow glass or ceramic platter and cover with plastic wrap until you want to serve it.

4. This is best served at room temperature.

Pasta Salad with Goat Cheese and Kalamata Olives, Salami & Fresh Basil

This pasta is extremely flavorful. I sometimes use this dish as a complete lunch or as an addition to a buffet table.

Ingredients

7 oz. dried <u>small</u> <u>shell</u> pasta, cooked until tender and drained

3 Tablespoons extra virgin olive oil

15 grape tomatoes, washed and halved

7 scallions, washed, roots removed and sliced very thinly. Use all of the white part and 3 inches of the green part

15 pitted Kalamata black olives, halved

6 oz. chunk of good tasting salami, just remove the "skin" and cut into <u>small</u> chunks

6 oz. goat cheese, crumbled

10 fresh basil leaves, washed, dried and snipped with kitchen scissors into thin strips

Dressing

1/3 cup balsamic vinegar

3 pinches ground cayenne pepper

1/2 teaspoon salt

1-1/2 cups extra virgin olive oil

Directions

1. While you're prepping the other ingredients, toss the drained pasta with the 3 Tablespoons of extra virgin olive oil in a large glass bowl. This will prevent it from sticking together.

2. Add all of the other ingredients to the bowl and stir gently until combined.

3. Pour the dressing over everything and stir gently until all of the pasta is coated.

4. Cover bowl with plastic wrap and refrigerate. It will take about 2 hours or more for all of the flavors to develop. So, it would be best to make it in the morning of the day you wanted it or even the day before.

5. For dressing, mix all ingredients together in a blender.

Salade Niçoise

A complete meal and beautiful, too!

Ingredients

2 lightly sautéed tuna steaks in extra virgin olive oil

3 medium sized peeled and cooked white potatoes (*not Idaho or Russet*). Slice these 3/4 inch thick

2 cups haricot verts (*skinny green beans*), steamed

4 hard boiled eggs, peeled and quartered

6 Campari tomatoes, quartered

30 Kalamata black olives, pitted

4 Tablespoons capers, drained and rinsed

1 small red onion, peeled and sliced very thinly

2 - 2 oz.cans flat anchovies, drained

Lettuce of your choice to line your platter

Directions

Use the largest glass or ceramic platter that you have. Arrange all of the ingredients around the tuna.

Shrimp, Crab or Lobster Salad

Ingredients

1 lb. cooked shrimp, crab or lobster meat, cut into bite-sized chunks

1 inner rib of celery, destrung and diced into tiny pieces

7 scallions, derooted and sliced thinly
(Use all of white part and 3 inches of green part)

1 Tablespoon freshly grated onion
(It will look like pulp)

1/2 cup good mayonnaise mixed with 3 Tablespoons light cream

2 Tablespoons fresh lime juice

Garnish

Wedges of fresh lime

Directions

1. Gently mix ingredients together in a medium sized glass bowl.

2. Serve in a glass or ceramic bowl and garnish with wedges of fresh lime.

Spinach, Bacon and Avocado Salad

Ingredients

3-4 oz. fresh baby spinach leaves, washed, spun dried and larger stems removed

1/2 pound bacon, cooked until crisp, drained on paper towels, then broken into large pieces

2 ripe Haas avocados

Juice of 1 lemon

3/4 cup good commercial creamy balsamic dressing (*I use Paul Newman's*)

Directions

1. Cut, peel and depit the avocados. Now slice them about 1/2 inch thick and rub each slice with some of the lemon juice. This will prevent the slices from turning brown.

2. Arrange the avocado slices over the spinach leaves.

3. Sprinkle the bacon over the top evenly.

4. Pour the dressing in a pitcher and pass separately. You do this so the salad doesn't get soggy.

Tomato, Mozzarella and Basil Salad

Ingredients

6 Campari tomatoes,
washed and quartered

1 lb. Mozzarella cheese, preferably
packed in water, sliced 1/4 inch thick
after draining

30 pitted Kalamata olives, halved

1 tin flat anchovy fillets, drained

1/2 cup fresh basil leaves, washed,
spun dried and torn into pieces

1/2 small red onion, peeled, halved
and sliced very thinly

Dressing

2-3 Tablespoons extra virgin olive oil

1 Tablespoon balsamic vinegar

1/2 teaspoon Kosher salt, maybe more

5-6 grinds fresh black peppercorns

Directions

1. Arrange all of the ingredients on a large glass or ceramic platter. Please do not mix the ingredients together.

2. Sprinkle dressing ingredients, one by one, evenly over the top of the salad.

About the Author

Annie Simensen has spent much of her life in kitchens: kitchens in the twenty-two homes and apartments around the world she's shared with her husband and daughter, and kitchens in schools where she honed her culinary technique and expertise with some of the top European and Asian instructors and chefs.

Annie's passion for food and cooking was ignited in the 4-H program in Long Island, NY. After graduating from college with a degree in education, she married her college sweetheart who was developing a complementary passion for fine wine. They regularly vacationed in Europe and enthusiastically explored regional cuisines and wines, more often in bistros and cafes than in 'starred' restaurants. Annie began what is now an immense collection of cookbooks and experimented with dishes not then common in American homes: squid cooked in its own ink, pressed tongue, garlic roasted quail, and slow, oven-roasted goose. Next, she began the process of developing recipes of her own creation, which, over the years, evolved into this series, *Annie's Elegant, Delicious Cooking.*

In the late seventies Annie's husband went to work for a British company; the family moved to England and began what would become an eighteen year journey around the world. In the little village of South Ascot, Annie befriended an elderly woman who had, for most of her life, been 'in service' in the kitchen of a Royal household. Under her tutelage, amongst other skills, Annie discovered how to perfect, 'Yorkshire Pudding,' and was entrusted with the secret recipe for the Duchess of Windsor's favorite chocolate dessert.

After finishing several, single topic courses at Le Cordon Bleu cooking school in London, Annie decided to enroll in the Cordon Bleu certificate course, the intensive course that prepares students for careers in the restaurant and food business. The course was both physically and academically demanding, but she passed the hands-on and written exams with flying colors and was awarded the Cordon Bleu Certificate, with honors. After graduation, Annie worked with a fellow student setting up a menu consulting service for up-scale London pubs.

The family's next move was to Tokyo where Annie studied for six months at the feet, (literally) of Kiyoko Konishi, the celebrated Japanese cooking instructor and TV personality. Annie made several appearances assisting Konishi-san on her weekly Japanese TV show. Regular trips to Tokyo's wholesale food markets and to the extensive food halls in major Japanese department stores broadened Annie's understanding of Japanese ingredients and both traditional and 'westernized' Japanese cuisine.

A move to Singapore followed. This time around, Annie decided that she would be the teacher rather than a student, and started her Singapore Cooking School. Annie's students came from many nations: South Africa, Australia, Hong Kong, Canada, Malaysia, Singapore, America and the Philippines. The focus was on preparing *Annie's Elegant, Delicious* meals for both entertaining guests and for family dinners and lunches. At each session, Annie's students worked as a group to create a complete meal and then sat down together for an early dinner with complementing wines. From the outset, Annie's school was completely booked with a steady waiting list.

Finally, Annie and her husband returned to their pre-revolutionary farm house in Massachusetts where she started to write *Annie's Elegant, Delicious Cooking.* Her writing was interrupted by a short assignment and relocation to Frankfurt, Germany where she prowled the restaurants and food markets around the country and added more knowledge of German regional cooking and specialty baking to her extensive, in-country experiences.

Springing from her life-long adventure with the pleasures of cooking, Annie has created a series of books that cooks at every level of experience can use to create *Annie's Elegant, Delicious* meals.

Salads

Copyright © 2012 by Annie Simensen

Photography by Carla Narrett

Book design, layout and image editing by Picturia Press (www.picturiapress.com)

16527288R00031

Made in the USA
Charleston, SC
26 December 2012